Healthy Roses

Environmentally Friendly Ways to Manage Pests and Disorders in Your Garden and Landscape

Second Edition

JOHN KARLIK
Horticultural Advisor, University of California
Cooperative Extension, Kern County

MARY LOUISE FLINT
Extension Entomologist, University of California, Davis, and
University of California Statewide IPM Program

DEBORAH GOLINO
Director, Foundation Plant Services
University of California, Davis

UNIVERSITY OF CALIFORNIA
Agriculture & Natural Resources

Publication 21589

Contents

Environmentally Friendly Ways to Manage Pests and Disorders in Your Garden and Landscape

Roses have had an undeserved reputation as temperamental, demanding plants with many pest problems, perhaps suitable for gardens but lacking the toughness required in low-maintenance landscapes. As a result, many gardeners may have assumed that maintenance of these beautiful plants requires frequent use of pesticides. On the other hand, a growing number of rose enthusiasts are able to produce high-quality blooms with little to no use of toxic materials, especially in California's dry interior valleys. This publication focuses on growing healthy roses with an understanding of pest biology and a resulting minimum of pesticide applications.

Roses in the landscape grow in an interrelated system that includes other plants, environmental conditions, pests, and other organisms. Through careful selection of plant varieties and management of environmental conditions with proper cultural practices, beautiful roses can be grown with a minimum of pest problems. Initial placement of roses into a suitable site gives the plants the best opportunity for growth with only occasional maintenance.

Once established, healthy roses provided with appropriate fertilizer and irrigation are less susceptible to many pest problems. Sanitation efforts such as picking up fallen leaves and winter pruning can contribute to reducing disease incidence in spring. Many insects can be hosed off with water, hand-picked, or pruned out. And, weeds can be managed with mulches and hand-weeding to reduce competition and provide an attractive landscape.

Insecticides, fungicides, and herbicides are effective tools for managing some pests, and their occasional use can be part of an integrated pest management (IPM) program for roses in the garden. However, increasing reliance on other management methods, together with careful selection of pesticide materials and timing of application, will reduce environmental impacts in the landscape.

This publication lists and illustrates the common pests and disorders of roses likely to occur in California and gives brief information on their management. Although the number of pests and disorders may seem large, many pests occur only in some areas of California, and only a few of these are likely to occur in any one garden. Although low levels of most pests require no treatment, it is important to be able to identify the problems in your garden, take action when appropriate, and recognize beneficial insects that may be found on your roses.

Figure 1. Roses in a traditional garden setting.

Cultivar Selection

oses have been cultivated in garden settings since antiquity, and Roman writings refer to use of rose flowers for decoration and fragrance. Perhaps the earliest specific use of roses as landscape plants in the United States occurred in the late 1800s and early 1900s. Hybrids of *Rosa rugosa* roses from China and Japan were extensively planted as hedges around farmsteads on the Great Plains. Although the flowers of *Rosa rugosa* cultivars are small, the ability of plants to survive, even in temperatures of −30°F, made them a welcome and colorful addition to the landscape.

Modern roses may be classified based on lineage and flowering characteristics. Hybrid teas and grandifloras were developed primarily for their large, showy flowers (fig. 1). Because of their profuse bloom and disease resistance, the cluster-flowered floribundas and polyanthas are more suitable for landscape use than hybrid teas and grandifloras. Selective hybridization with incorporation of floribunda parentage has resulted in the relatively recent development of landscape roses, also called shrub roses, which are cultivars selected specifically for use as flowering shrubs in the landscape. These varieties incorporate enhanced disease and insect resistance and require less pruning than traditional garden varieties of roses. Their planting and care is also easier because their thorns are smaller and less numerous than those found on traditional varieties. Because petals and spent flowers separate from the stems, deadheading (removing old flowers) is not required. In cold weather areas, the own-root propagation of landscape roses means that plants can regenerate true to

Figure 2. Upright landscape rose varieties are medium to large shrubs. Shown here is 'Pink Simplicity.'

type even if they are killed to the ground by cold temperatures.

Landscape roses are available in three growth forms: upright plants, mounding shrub roses, and ground covers.

- *Upright plants* grow as medium-to-large shrubs with uniform foliage and bloom (fig. 2). These varieties can be used as border plantings, screens, or for vertical accents in a landscape design. Multiple plantings can be maintained as an informal hedge. Varieties include 'Flutterbye,' 'Pink Meidiland,' 'Sevillana,' and 'Simplicity.'

- *Mounding shrub* roses are more rambling than upright varieties (fig. 3). Uses include borders and mass plantings. Varieties include 'Bonica,' 'Lady of the Dawn,' 'Lavender Dream,' 'Knock Out,' and 'Scarlet Meidiland.'

- *Ground covers* are low-growing varieties that are useful as covers for sloping banks, borders for walkways, or cascades over walls (fig. 4). Some varieties reach $2\frac{1}{2}$ feet in height. Varieties include 'Alba Meidiland,' 'Baby Blanket,' 'Carefree Delight,' 'Eyeopener,' 'The Fairy,' 'Flower Carpet,' 'Ralph's Creeper,' 'Red Ribbons,' 'Red Meidiland,' and 'Sea Foam.'

Figure 3. Mounding landscape shrub roses are more rambling than upright varieties. The variety shown is 'Wild Dancer.'

Figure 4. Groundcover roses, such as 'Ralph's Creeper' shown here, are useful for covering banks or walls.

Cultural Practices

Establishment

Roses are often purchased in late winter or early spring as bare-root plants. To maintain plant health prior to sale, these plants should be held in the nursery under cool conditions with their roots kept moist. Packaged plants should also be kept cool because warm temperatures hasten loss of carbohydrate reserves and contribute to gradual desiccation of wood and the resulting difficulty in establishment. Establishment from bare-root stock becomes more difficult as day temperatures rise above 70°F in late spring. To increase the percentage of survival when planting bare-root stock in May or June, mist the wood once or twice per day and place mulch around the base of the plant to increase humidity.

Roses may be planted throughout the summer from nursery containers. However, the current season's stock is to be preferred rather than container stock held over from the previous year. With the exception of miniatures and smaller cultivars, roses generally do not perform well when maintained in nursery pots for more than one season.

Planting sites may have full sun to partial shade; however, roses do best with 6 hours or more of direct sun per day.

Irrigation

Roses need to be irrigated in most locations in California. Drought stress leads to defoliation and sunburn of canes and may contribute to spider mite problems. However, overwatering or poorly drained soils may lead to root disease and nutritional deficiencies. Frequency and duration of irrigation depend on weather conditions and soil texture. Roses do best when 50 percent of available water is depleted between irrigations. Checking after irrigation to determine the soil moisture status and rate of depletion is helpful in scheduling irrigation. Daily irrigation should not be necessary even in the desert areas of California. For example, in the Central Valley, rose plants in production fields are irrigated, at most, at 8-day intervals during the warmest months, and irrigation twice per week is usually satisfactory for roses in landscapes. Water may be supplied via overhead sprays, flood irrigation, or drip tubing. Irrigation with over-the-top delivery should take place in the morning so foliage dries during the day. Mulches help decrease water loss from the soil through evaporation and may enhance growth of the root system.

Soil and Nutritional Requirements

Roses prefer well-drained soil with a pH near the neutral value of 7.0. Many California soils are still suitable despite a pH above 7.0, but the likelihood of micronutrient deficiencies becomes greater as pH increases, especially for pH values above 7.5. Roses are not salt tolerant, so electrical conductivity (EC_e) values, which describe the concentration of salt ions in the soil, should be less than 2.0 decisiemens

Table 1. Suggested soil pH, EC_e, and nutrient levels for roses.

Soil Characteristics	Units	Low	High
pH (acidity/alkalinity)	ó	6.0	7.5
ECe (electrical conductivity)	dS/m	0.5	2.0
NO3-N (nitrate-N)	ppm	35	150
NH4-N (ammoniacal-N)	ppm	0	20
P (phosphorus)	ppm	5	50
K (potassium)	ppm	50	300
Ca (calcium)	ppm	40	200
Mg (magnesium)	ppm	20	100
B (boron)	ppm	0.1	0.75
Fe (iron)	ppm	0.3	3.0
Mn (manganese)	ppm	0.2	3.0
Cu (copper)	ppm	0.001	0.5
Zn (zinc)	ppm	0.03	3.0
Mo (molybdenum)	ppm	0.01	0.10

per meter (dS/m). Soil test values suitable for roses are given in table 1.

Nitrogen is the nutrient typically in shortest supply. Although soil nitrate (NO_3-N) levels may be lower than the suggested soil test value, this nutrient is easy to add, so a low soil supply of NO_3-N is usually not problematic. For young landscape plantings or home gardens, adding nitrogen at the rate of 1 pound of actual nitrogen per 1,000 square feet twice per year, spring and fall, should provide an adequate amount of this nutrient. Slow-release fertilizers may be used. For sandy soils and for soluble fertilizers, splitting the seasonal application into two parts 1 month apart is suggested. For mature plantings, adding nitrogen only in the spring may be sufficient. Too much nitrogen may shift plants into vegetative growth at the expense of flowers.

Although tissue tests are not normally needed for roses in landscape settings, they may be used to provide information on the current nutritional status of the rose plant. Suggested nutrient levels are presented in table 2.

Table 2. Suggested values for nutrient levels in rose tissue.

Nutrient (unit)	Low	High
N (%)	3.0	5.0
P (%)	0.2	0.3
K (%)	2.0	3.0
Ca (%)	1.0	1.5
Mg (%)	0.25	0.35
Zn (ppm)	15	50
Mn (ppm)	30	250
Fe (ppm)	50	150
Cu (ppm)	5	15
B (ppm)	30	60

Pruning

Pruning provides an opportunity to direct growth and invigorate rose plants. Pruning requirements vary among types of rose plants. Hybrid teas, grandifloras, and many floribundas benefit from annual pruning in which most top growth is removed, leaving three to five canes in a vase-shaped configuration (fig. 5). Landscape varieties may be hedged or left unpruned, although rejuvenation pruning or removal of older stems every 2 to 3 years renews vigor in the planting. In most of California, pruning should be done in winter before buds swell, although it may be delayed where late spring frosts

Figure 5. A vase-shaped configuration is the goal when pruning.

are common. A starting point in pruning is to remove diseased and damaged wood. Between one-third and two-thirds of healthy wood may be removed through a combination of heading and thinning cuts, which should be within $\frac{1}{4}$ inch above outwardly growing lateral buds or branches (fig. 6). Removal of more wood results in fewer but larger flowers with longer stems; less pruning preserves the size of plants and results in a greater number of smaller flowers. Pruning paint or other wound dressing is not necessary.

During the growing season, the rule of thumb for cutting blooms on first-year plants is to make the cut above the first outwardly facing five-leaflet leaf. On well-established plants, cut blooms somewhat lower to ensure that new canes can support the weight of the blooms. Removal of spent rose blossoms (deadheading) allows the plant to conserve energy and leads to further flower production. To deadhead a rose plant, use the same guidelines as for cutting blooms. Landscape varieties do not need to be deadheaded.

Figure 6. Pruning cuts should be made cleanly above a lateral bud (arrow) or branch.

Weed Management

Weeds are common in many landscape situations, including around rose plantings. Mulching with 2 to 4 inches of organic material such as wood chips helps reduce annual weeds and makes hand-weeding easier. Woven landscape fabric placed under organic mulch provides weed control for several years. In most home gardens, mulches supplemented with regular hand-weeding or rogueing (digging out the entire weed plant, roots and all) should provide satisfactory weed control. Mechanical cultivation devices such as hoes must be used with care because roses are shallow rooted.

In extensive plantings or professionally managed public or commercial landscapes, mulches and hand-weeding may be supplemented with herbicides. Some of these materials may be available only to professional applicators and not to home gardeners. The preemergent herbicides oryzalin (Surflan) and pendimethalin (Pendulum) can be used around roses before weeds emerge or after weeds are removed, but before others germinate. While these herbicides control primarily grasses, they also control broadleaf plants such as chickweed, fiddleneck, knotweed, lambsquarters, pigweed, prostrate spurge, oxalis (from seed), and purslane. These herbicides do not control established weeds. To control established grasses, the postemergent herbicides fluazifop-p-butyl (Fusilade), sethoxydim (Sethoxydim), and clethodim (Envoy) may be used when the grass plants are small; when these herbicides are used according to label directions they do not injure rose plants. Be sure to consult labels for permitted sites and rates.

Roses are sensitive to postemergent broadleaf herbicides used in the landscape such as 2,4-D, mecoprop, triclopyr, and dicamba. Use broadleaf herbicides with great care when rose plants are present in the landscape so as to not cause damage from drift. Roses are also very sensitive to glyphosate (Roundup and many other trade names), which can be absorbed through the green stems in addition to the leaves. Glyphosate damage may appear at bud break the following spring after a summer or fall application that contacts leaves or stems; symptoms include a proliferation of small, narrow shoots and leaves. For more information on weed control in the landscape, see *Pest Notes: Weed Management in Landscapes* (Wilen and Elmore 2007; see the references).

Although insects and mites may attack roses from time to time, many rose enthusiasts are able to maintain vigorous plants and produce high-quality blooms with little or no use of insecticides, especially in California's dry interior valleys. The keys to success are careful selection of varieties, good attention to appropriate cultural practices, and occasional handpicking or using water to forcefully spray away pests. Keep an eye out for rising populations of natural enemies that often rapidly reduce the numbers of aphids, mites, and other pests.

Common Insect and Mite Pests

Aphids. Aphids are the most common insect pest on roses. The actual aphid species present depends on where in the state the roses are grown. These may include the rose aphid (*Macrosiphum rosae*) (fig. 7), the potato aphid (*Macrosiphum euphorbiae*), and the cotton aphid (*Aphis gossypii*), among others. Aphids favor rapidly growing tissue such as buds and shoots. Low to moderate levels of aphids do little damage to plants, although many gardeners are concerned with their very presence. Moderate to high populations can secrete copious amounts of honeydew, resulting in the growth of sooty mold, which blackens leaves. Very high numbers may distort or kill buds or reduce flower size. In most areas of California aphids are normally a problem for only about 4 to 6 weeks in spring and early summer before high summer temperatures reduce their numbers.

Aphids have many natural enemies, including lady beetles, soldier beetles, and syrphid flies (see the section "Common Natural Enemies of Insect and Mite Pests in California"), which may rapidly reduce increasing populations. Ants protect aphid populations against natural enemies to obtain their honeydew. Keep ants out of bushes with sticky barriers, baits, or traps to

Insect and Mite Pests and Beneficials

Figure 7. Rose aphids *(Macrosiphum rosae).*

improve biological control. Lady beetles often increase in number when aphid populations are high. The convergent lady beetle is sold at nurseries for release against aphids and may provide temporary control when properly released. Releasing green lacewings against the rose aphid has not been shown to offer significant control in research trials. A naturally occurring disease may control aphids when conditions are wet or humid (fig. 8).

In many landscape situations, knocking aphids off with a forceful spray of water early in the day is all that is needed to supplement natural control. Insecticidal soaps or neem oil can also be used to increase mortality of aphids with only moderate impact on natural enemies. Soil-applied systemic insecticides, such as imidacloprid (a home garden product with this ingredient is sold under the Bayer label), are effective but are not usually necessary. Use of more toxic products is not warranted in most gardens and landscapes.

Insects and Mites That Cause Leaves to Stipple or Yellow

Spider mites, including two-spotted mite, Pacific mite, and strawberry mite, all *Tetranychus* spp., cause leaves to be stippled or bleached (figs. 9 and 10) and may cause leaves to dry up and fall off. Some species produce webbing while others do not. These mites are tiny (about the size of the period at the end of this sentence) and are best seen with use of a hand lens.

Mites usually appear first on the undersides of leaves but move to the upper sides as populations

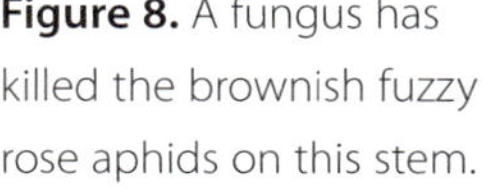

Figure 8. A fungus has killed the brownish fuzzy rose aphids on this stem.

Figure 9. Spider mites have caused the stippling on these leaves.

Figure 10. A two-spotted spider mite *(Tetranychus urticae)* (bottom) and its predator, the western predatory mite *(Galendromus* [= *Metasieulus*] *occidentalis)* (top). The eggs are those of the two-spotted spider mite.

increase. High numbers are usually associated with dry, dusty conditions. Spider mite numbers may greatly increase if their many natural enemies are killed by broad-spectrum insecticides applied for other pests. For instance, applications of carbaryl (Sevin) applied to control other pests are frequently followed by an increase in mite populations.

Conserving natural enemies, providing sufficient irrigation, and reducing dust may help control mites. Overhead irrigation or periodic washing of leaves with water can be very effective in reducing mite numbers. Releases of predator mites have been used in some situations.

If treatment is necessary, spider mites can be controlled with insecticidal soap, horticultural oil, or neem oil, and sprays should be targeted to ensure coverage on the undersides of the leaves. Although spider mites may be listed on insecticide labels, most insecticides are not very effective against them and can trigger mite flare-ups as mentioned above. Selective acaricides (miticides) are often difficult to find in the home garden market.

Rose leafhopper *(Edwardsianna rosae)* (fig. 11) causes stippling larger than mite stippling but tends to be a problem only in certain localities. Along with stippling, cast skins and the absence of webbing on the underside of leaves are good indications that these pests are present. Plants can tolerate moderate stippling. Use an insecticidal soap if an infestation is severe.

Insects That Distort or Discolor Blossoms

Thrips. Western flower thrips (*Frankliniella occidentalis*) (fig. 12) and Madrone thrips (*Thrips madroni*) cause injury primarily to rose flowers, causing blossom petals to streak with brown or become distorted (fig. 13), and flowers can be particularly damaged if attacked early at the bud stage. The tiny yellow or black thrips insects can be found within the blossoms.

Thrips damage is more likely to be severe where many rose bushes located close together provide a continuously blooming habitat. Fragrant, light-colored or white roses are most often attacked and can be severely damaged. Cultivars with sepals that remain tightly wrapped around the bud until blooms open have fewer problems. In most home garden and landscape situations, thrips can be tolerated. Frequent clipping and disposal of spent blooms may reduce thrips problems. Control with insecticides is difficult because materials are mostly effective on early developmental stages, which are commonly found within buds or flowers where most pesticide applications cannot penetrate. It should be noted that western flower thrips can have a beneficial role as a predator of spider mites.

Figure 11. The rose leafhopper *(Edwardsianna rosae)* may occasionally cause leaf stippling that is somewhat larger than that of spider mites.

Figure 12. The western flower thrips *(Frankliniella occidentalis)* is frequently found in blossoms.

Figure 13. The western flower thrips may cause brownish scarring on sepals.

Insects That May Chew Blossoms or Leaves

Fuller rose beetle (*Asynonychus godmani*) (fig. 14) adults chew flowers and foliage, leaving notched or ragged edges (fig. 15). Adults are pale brown weevils that are about ⅜ inch long. They are flightless and hide during the day, often on the underside of leaves; feeding takes place at night. The larvae are root feeders but do not seriously damage roses.

Low numbers can be ignored; otherwise, hand-pick the beetles off the plant, use sticky material on stems, and trim branches that create bridges to walls and other plants. The adults are difficult to control with insecticides because they have a long emergence period, from June to November. Parasitic nematodes may be helpful if applied to the soil in early to midsummer.

Hoplia beetle (*Hoplia callipyge*) (fig. 16) is about ¼ inch long and chews holes mostly in the petals of open flowers. It is primarily a problem in the Central Valley from Sacramento south to Bakersfield. The hoplia beetle prefers feeding on light-colored roses (white, pink, apricot, and yellow) but does not damage leaves. Larvae are root feeders but do not feed on the roots of rose plants. There is only one generation per year, and damage is usually confined to

Figure 14. The Fuller rose beetle *(Asynonychus godmani)* is a robust brown weevil just under a half inch long.

Figure 15. Fuller rose beetles chew flowers and foliage, leaving notched or ragged edges.

Figure 16. The hoplia beetle *(Hoplia callipyge)* chews holes mostly in petals of open flowers.

a 2- to 4-week period in late spring.

Adult hoplia beetles can be hand-picked, or infested rose blooms may be clipped off plants. Sprays are not very effective and should not be necessary in a garden situation. Although there is a resemblance, Japanese beetles *(Popillia japonica)* have not been reported in California.

Leafcutter bees *(Megachile* spp.) cut semicircular holes in the margins of leaves (fig. 17) and carry leaf material back to use in lining their nests. Bees are important pollinators and should not be killed. Tolerate this pest as there are no effective controls.

Figure 17. Leafcutter bees *(Megachile* spp.) cut circular holes in the margins of leaves.

Figure 18. Caterpillars may occasionally bore into buds, leaving a large hole. Look for the caterpillar inside.

Figure 19. When a bud bored by a caterpillar opens, the petals will be chewed and frass may be visible.

Rose curculio (*Merhynchites* spp.), is a red to black snout weevil about ¼ inch long that prefers yellow and white roses. It punches holes in flowers and buds and may create ragged holes in blossoms or kill the developing bud. If weevils are numerous, terminal shoots may be killed as well. Larvae feed within buds, often killing them before they open. Hand-pick adults off plants and destroy infested buds. A broad-spectrum insecticide can be applied to kill adults if the infestation is severe.

Caterpillars such as orange tortrix, tussock moth, fruittree leafroller, tent caterpillar, and omnivorous looper may feed on rose leaves; some of these caterpillars may also tie leaves with silk. Damage is usually not severe and treatment is not usually necessary. Hand-pick or clip out rolled leaves. Small leaf-feeding caterpillars can be killed with an application of

Figure 20. The adult of the bristly roseslug (*Cladius difformis*) is a sawfly in the order Hymenoptera.

the microbial insecticides *Bacillus thuringiensis* or spinosad. Some caterpillars, like the tobacco budworm, may occasionally bore into flower buds (figs. 18 and 19). Look for the caterpillar or its frass inside. Prune out and destroy damaged buds.

Rose slug (*Endelomyia aethiops*) is the black to pale green, sluglike larva of a sawfly (fig. 20). Unlike pear slug, this species has apparent legs and looks like a caterpillar. Young larvae skeletonize the lower leaf surface, while mature larvae chew large holes in leaves (fig. 21). These pests have many natural enemies. They may be washed off with a strong stream of water or killed with an application of insecticidal soap or spinosad. *Bacillus thuringiensis* will not work because these are wasp larvae and not the larvae of butterflies or moths.

Figure 21. This bristly roseslug larva has chewed large holes in a leaf. The presence of prolegs on all its abdominal segments distinguishes it from caterpillars.

Figure 22. The larva of a flatheaded borer (family Buprestidae) feeding beneath the bark.

Figure 23. A raspberry horntail *(Hartigia cressoni)* larva feeding in a rose cane.

Figure 24. Raspberry horntail can cause tips of canes to wilt and die. Prune out horntail-infested canes.

Insects That Cause Canes to Die Back

Flatheaded borers (*Chrysobothris* spp.) (fig. 22) may kill canes or an entire plant. Larvae are white and up to 1 inch long with enlarged heads. Adult beetles do not significantly damage roses. Eggs tend to be laid on stressed rose plants, especially in bark wounds caused by sunburn or disease. Remove and destroy infested material and keep plants healthy by providing sufficient irrigation and avoiding excessive summer pruning.

Raspberry horntail (*Hartigia cressoni*) (fig. 23) larvae are white segmented caterpillars up to 1 inch long that can cause tips of canes to wilt and die in spring (fig. 24), reducing second-cycle blooms. Adults appear wasplike, black or black and yellow, and about 1/2 inch long. Inspect canes in spring (mid-April to mid-June) for egg-laying incisions or swellings caused by larvae and cut them off below the infestation. Prune off infested canes until healthy pith is found.

Scale insects include the armored scales rose scale (*Aulacaspis rosae*) and San Jose scale (*Quadraspidiotus perniciosus*). These may cause cane decline or dieback when numbers are high. San Jose scale may spread by wind from almond orchards, and so may be found on roses near the urban-agricultural transition in California's Central Valley. These armored scales can be observed on canes as small, grayish, round to oval encrustations, ranging in size from 1/8 to 1/4 inch. These insects have no legs or antennae for most of their lives and are immobile.

In winter, cut back and destroy infested canes and apply insecticidal oil to remaining infested canes if remaining scale population is high. Scales are attacked by many natural enemies. Look for exit holes in mature scale covers, which indicate parasitization.

A soft scale, cottony cushion scale *(Icerya purchasi)*, may also be found on roses. Soft scales produce honeydew that may cause leaves to be sticky and allow sooty mold to colonize leaf surfaces. Washing plants with soap and water may reduce the population. Pruning and application of horticultural oil as for armored scales should provide sufficient control.

Insects Seldom Found in California

Mossy rose gall *(Diplolepis rosae)* causes a spherical spined mass of plant tissue about 1 inch in diameter to form on year-old rose twigs. At first the deformity resembles moss but becomes hardened as it enlarges. The causal insect is a gall wasp. A related insect causes an elongated stem gall to form, and about forty different kinds of galls can form on rose twigs. These galls are more common in cooler, northern parts of California than in the Central Valley. Pruning should provide sufficient control.

Rose midge *(Dasineura rhodophaga)* was reported infesting roses in a nursery in Petaluma, California, in August 1996. Rose midges are tiny flies that lay their eggs inside the sepals of flower buds or on plant terminals. Hatching larvae move into flower buds to feed, leaving the injured buds to wither, blacken, and die. Pupation occurs in the soil, and two to four generations can occur annually. When first reported in 1996, there was widespread fear that this pest would move rapidly through the state, causing severe damage to roses in gardens and commercial nurseries. However, few midges have been found in California since 1997. The pest has been present in central Oregon and Washington for many years and is not known to be a major pest there. Hopefully it will not become a problem in California. Take any suspected infested material to your county agricultural commissioner for identification. Do not confuse the rose midge with the similar-looking beneficial midge *Aphidoletes aphidimyza* (fig. 25), which feeds on aphids. *Aphidoletes* larvae are found on stem, bud, or leaf surfaces feeding within aphid colonies (fig. 26), whereas *Dasineura* larvae are out of view at the base of developing buds in terminals.

Figure 25. (top) *Aphidoletes aphidimyza* is a beneficial midge that resembles the rose midge.

Figure 26. (bottom) An *Aphidoletes* larva feeding on aphids.

Common Natural Enemies of Insect and Mite Pests in Roses

Figure 27. Parasitized aphids crust over and form bronze or black mummies. A tiny parasitic wasp will emerge from this aphid.

Aphid parasites. Tiny parasitic wasps are very important in the control of aphids in roses. Adults lay their eggs within the aphid and developing wasp larvae rapidly immobilize the aphids. Eventually, the parasite kills them and turns them into bronze or black crusty, bloated mummies (fig. 27). The parasite pupates within the mummy and then cuts a neat round hole and emerges as a full-grown wasp. Once you see one mummy in the aphid colony, you are likely to see more. Parasitic wasps are also important in the control of scale insects, caterpillars, and many other insect pests.

Minute pirate bug. Minute pirate bugs (*Orius tristicolor*) (fig. 28) are tiny true bugs with black and white markings as adults. They are often among the first predators to appear in spring, and they feed on mites, insect and mite eggs, immature scales, and thrips.

Figure 28. The minute pirate bug *(Orius tristicolor)* is a common predator of mites, thrips, and insect eggs. As its name indicates, it is tiny.

Figure 29. This green lacewing (*Chrysoperla* spp.) larva is feeding on a rose aphid.

Figure 30. The convergent lady beetle (*Hippodamia convergens*) is the most common lady beetle in gardens. Pictured here are three forms of the same species, showing spotless and spotted forms.

Lacewings. Green lacewings in the genera *Chrysopa* and *Chrysoperla* (fig. 29) are common natural enemies of aphids and other soft-bodied insects. |The gray-green to brown alligator-shaped larvae are the predatory stage of the *Chrysoperla* species. The green lacy-winged adults feed on honeydew.

Lady beetles. Many different red and black lady beetle species are predators of aphids; the most common is the convergent lady beetle (*Hippodamia convergens*) (figs. 30 and 31).

Figure 31. The larva of the convergent lady beetle has distinct legs, a tapered abdomen, and orange spots.

Figure 32. The multicolored Asian lady beetle *(Harmonia axyridis)* is becoming more common in California gardens.

Another common species in the garden is the multicolored lady beetle *(Harmonia axyridis)* (fig. 32). These lady beetles have the advantage of feeding primarily on aphids and are predators in both the adult and larval stages. Look for the black, alligator-shaped larva with orange dots and the oblong, yellow eggs that are laid on end in groups.

Releases of commercially available convergent lady beetles can reduce aphid numbers. However, large numbers must be released on each individual rose plant. Mist lady beetles with a water spray before release. Make releases in the evening at dusk by placing beetles on canes at the base of plants. Wet plants first with a fine spray of water. Expect 90 percent of the lady beetles to fly away in the first 24 hours. The remaining lady beetles are unlikely to lay eggs and will fly

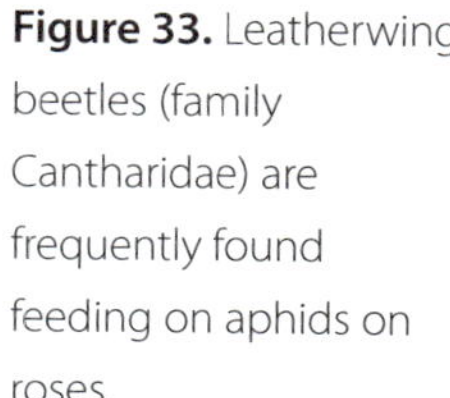

Figure 33. Leatherwing beetles (family Cantharidae) are frequently found feeding on aphids on roses.

away once aphid populations have been substantially reduced.

Leatherwings or soldier beetles. These moderate to large beetles in the Cantharid family have leatherlike dark wings and orange or red heads and thoraxes (fig. 33). They feed on aphids and are very common on roses. Many people mistake them for pests, but they are predaceous both as adults and larvae (in the soil). Sometimes they leave dark splotches of excrement on leaves.

Syrphid flies. Syrphids, sometimes called flower flies or hover flies, are important predators of aphids and are very common on roses. Syrphids superficially resemble wasps, feed on nectar and pollen before reproducing, and are often seen hovering above flowers (fig. 34). Larvae, often found within aphid colonies, are legless and maggot

Figure 34. The syrphid fly adult (family Syrphidae) has a striped abdomen and often hovers around flowers.

Figure 35. This syrphid fly larva is one of many species that feeds on rose aphids.

shaped (fig. 35). There are many species in California; they vary in color from dull brown or yellow to bright green, but most have a yellow longitudinal stripe on the back. Do not mistake them for moth or butterfly larvae.

Predaceous mites. A number of predatory mites feed on spider mites, often keeping them at tolerable levels. Predatory mites can be distinguished from the plant-feeding spider mites by the absence of the two spots on either side of the body, their pear shape, and their more active habits. Compared to the plant-feeding species of mites that remain in one location feeding, predatory mites move rapidly around the leaf when looking for prey. Because they are so small, a hand lens is helpful in viewing them.

Thrips. Six-spotted thrips feeds on spider mites and is not a plant feeder. Western flower thrips are plant feeders but also feed on spider mites. While thrips damage cannot be tolerated in greenhouse production, in the field thrips often provide benefit exceeding the limited damage they cause.

Spiders. All spiders are predators and many contribute significantly to biological control. Many types of spiders, including crab spiders, jumping spiders, cobweb spiders, and the orb-weavers, occur in landscapes (fig. 36).

Figure 36. This black and yellow garden spider is one of many species of spiders that feed on pests in the rose garden.

Diseases and Abiotic Disorders

A variety of plant pathogens can attack roses, but rose cultivars vary significantly in susceptibility to disease problems. The most common problem in California is powdery mildew, but a number of other diseases including rust, black spot, botrytis, downy mildew, and anthracnose may cause problems where moist conditions prevail.

To limit problems, choose varieties and irrigation practices carefully, promote air circulation by following appropriate pruning techniques and providing sufficient space between plants, and remove severely infested material promptly. Although some rose enthusiasts consider regular application of fungicides a necessary component of rose culture, many gardeners are able to sustain plants with little to no use of fungicides, especially in California's dry interior valleys.

In addition to diseases that bacterial, fungal, and viral pathogens cause, roses may display similar damage symptoms resulting from chemical toxicities, mineral deficiencies, or environmental problems. Such problems are termed abiotic disorders, and changing environmental conditions often can correct these symptoms.

Symptoms on Leaves and Shoots

Powdery mildew, caused by the fungus *Podosphaera* (previously *Sphaerotheca*) *pannosa* var. *rosae,* produces white to gray powdery growth on leaves, shoots, sepals, buds, and occasionally on petals (fig. 37). Leaves may distort and drop.

Powdery mildew does not require free water on plant surfaces in order to develop and is active during California's warm, dry summers. Overhead sprinkling, such as irrigation or washing, during midday may limit the disease by disrupting the daily spore-release cycle, yet it allows time for foliage to dry before evening.

The pathogen requires living tissue in order to survive, so pruning, collecting, and disposing of leaves during the dormant season can limit infestations, although it may not entirely eradicate them, since airborne spores from other locations can provide fresh inoculation.

Rose varieties vary greatly in resistance, with landscape (shrub) varieties among the most resistant. Glossy-foliaged varieties of hybrid teas and grandifloras often have good resistance to powdery mildew as well. Plants grown in sunny locations with good air circulation are less likely to have serious problems.

Fungicides such as triforine (Ortho Rosepride or other trade names) are available, but generally must be applied to prevent rather than eradicate infections, so timing is critical and repeat applications may be necessary. In addition to synthetic fungicides, natural products with fungicidal activity are available, including horticultural oils, neem oil, jojoba oil, sulfur, potassium bicarbonate, and the biological fungicide Serenade. With the exception of the oils, these materials are primarily preventive, although potassium bicarbonate has some eradicant activity. Oils work best as eradicants but also have

Figure 37. Powdery mildew on a rose.

some protectant activity. Do not apply oils to water-stressed plants or within 2 weeks of a sulfur spray.

See the Pest Note *Powdery Mildew on Ornamentals* for more details on management.

Downy mildew, caused by the fungus *Peronospora sparsa,* requires a narrow range of temperature and humidity to thrive. Interveinal, angular purple, red, or brown spots appear on leaves, which then become yellow and drop (fig. 38). You occasionally may observe fruiting bodies of the fungus on the undersides of leaves.

To reduce downy mildew, increase air circulation through pruning and avoid frequent overhead irrigation that results in foliage that stays wet. Control with fungicides is very difficult; environmental management is much more likely to be effective. Because downy mildew requires moist, humid conditions, it is most likely to cause problems in coastal areas of California and, during a narrow period of time in spring and fall, in the Central Valley.

Rust, caused by the fungus *Phragmidium mucronatum* (formerly *P. disciflorum*), prefers cool, moist weather such as that found in coastal areas of California but also may be a problem inland during wet years. Infected plants have small orange pustules on the undersides of leaves while the upper sides of leaves may discolor and drop (fig. 39).

Avoid overhead watering and prune back severely affected canes. During the winter collect and dispose of any leaves remaining on the plants and those that have fallen off. Plants can tolerate low levels of damage without significant losses. You

Figure 38. Downy mildew on a rose leaf.

Figure 39. Rose rust appears as reddish brown spots on the lower leaf surface (left and bottom) and as yellow patches on the upper leaf surface (right).

can use preventive applications of fungicides, but it may require frequent applications to attempt to keep plants rust free, which may not be justifiable in garden or landscape situations.

Black spot, caused by the fungus *Diplocarpon rosae,* produces black spots with feathery or fibrous margins on the upper surfaces of leaves and stems (fig. 40). Small, black fruiting bodies are often present in spots on the upper sides of leaves. No fungal growth occurs on the undersides.

This fungus requires free water to reproduce and grow, so do not allow leaves to remain wet for more than 7 hours. Hose off aphids in the morning or midday, so leaves have a chance to dry before evening. Provide good air circulation around plants. Remove fallen leaves and other infested material, and prune out infected stems during the dormant season.

Black spot usually is not a problem in most of California. Miniature roses are more susceptible than other types, although a few varieties are reliably resistant to all strains of black spot. Apply fungicides such as chlorothalonil or triforine as preventatives. Horticultural oils, neem oil, potassium bicarbonate, and sulfur, as discussed above for powdery mildew, have been shown to be effective in reducing black spot.

Anthracnose, caused by the fungus *Sphaceloma rosarum,* results in leaf spots. When first formed, spots are red or sometimes brown to purple. Later the centers turn gray or white and have a dark red margin. Fruiting bodies may appear in the middle of the spot, and the lesion may fall out creating a shot-hole symptom.

Figure 40. Black spot causes dark blotches and yellowing.

Figure 41. Mosaic Viruses cause splotches or zigzag patterns on leaves.

No information on management is available. Hybrid teas and old-fashioned climbing and rambler roses are the most affected.

Viruses and viruslike diseases occur wherever roses grow, although damage may be mostly cosmetic with little reduction in plant vigor.

Rose mosaic disease (RMD) is named after the leaf symptoms infected roses display. Ringspots, line patterns, mosaics, and distortion or puckering are typical (figs. 41 and 42). Leaf symptoms depend on which virus or viruses are present, the rose cultivar, the time of year, and growing conditions. Color break on flowers also can be symptomatic of rose mosaic disease.

Figure 42. Some rose mosaic viruses cause ringspot patterns on leaves.

Visual symptoms also can be transient; for example, hot, bright days can cause the symptoms to appear milder or disappear. The virus remains and the plant becomes a symptomless carrier.

RMD is the result of an infection with a number of different viruses, the most common *Prunus necrotic ringspot virus* and *Apple mosaic virus*. *Arabis mosaic virus* also can cause RMD. These viruses may be present alone or in various combinations, accounting in part for the array of symptoms observed on infected plants. An accurate diagnosis may require laboratory tests and biological indexing.

A group of diseases of unknown causes that mimic some of the symptoms of mosaic have been discovered in California and other parts of the United States. These diseases include rose ring pattern, rose spring dwarf (RSD), and rose leaf curl. RSD causes rosetting or a balled appearance in the new growth following bud break. The leaves first emerging in the spring are recurved or very short and show conspicuous vein clearing or a netted appearance. These symptoms become less apparent as shoots eventually elongate. Canes may develop a zigzag pattern of growth as the season progresses. Recent studies have associated a new virus with this condition; for more information, see Salem et al. 2008 (listed in the references).

Viruses present many problems to commercial rose growers. Rose gardeners, retailers, and regulatory officials object to the symptoms. Cut flower producers may see a significant decrease in production and bloom quality, depending on the variety of rose and type of virus. Nursery plant producers may face rejection of interstate shipments; destruction may become severe enough that large numbers of plants become unsalable.

For homeowners, the problem largely is unsightly foliage, with possible decreased plant vigor and smaller, fewer flowers.

The most common causes for the spread of these viruses are propagation procedures such as budding an infected scion onto a healthy understock or a healthy scion to an infected understock. Disease symptoms are not always obvious, which is why the use of virus-tested planting stock is advantageous. Some evidence indicates that rose mosaic spreads in commercial rose plantings via root grafts.

Many rose catalogs and books refer to "virus-free" roses. The science of plant virology has shown in recent years that most horticultural plants have cryptic viruses in them, the function and importance of which are not known. As more sophisticated virus-testing techniques have been developed, many "virus-free" programs discovered that their stock was not as free of viruses as thought.

Foundation Plant Services (FPS) at UC Davis uses the term "virus tested" or "specific virus tested," meaning that the plant material has been tested for the specific viruses known to cause rose mosaic disease. FPS currently employs two virus elimination techniques, heat therapy and meristem tissue culture, to reestablish a rose cultivar without the virus pathogens. Both are slow, time-consuming processes. Worldwide, plant material that has been tested for and found free of viruses known to cause disease symptoms is referred to as "clean stock."

For the home rose grower, no effective method exists for eliminating the viruses that cause rose mosaic disease. Use of virus-indexed

Figure 43. Nitrogen deficiency has caused these lower rose leaves to develop interveinal chlorosis, a yellowing effect that occurs between the veins while the veins themselves remain green. The virus-infested upper leaves exhibit a condition known as pale vein clearing.

stock—plants that have tested negative for these viruses by laboratory and field methods—for field propagation is the recommended preventative practice.

Nutrient deficiencies cause specific symptoms such as leaves that yellow and older leaves that drop (fig. 43). Because many California soils have low percentages of organic matter, the nitrogen reserve typically is low, so you should add this nutrient as inorganic fertilizer or from organic sources.

Micronutrient deficiencies, especially iron and zinc, appear as interveinal chlorosis of new leaves. These elements may be deficient because soils are too wet or too alkaline or because the soil type, such as sandy loam, is low in micronutrient content. Because inorganic forms of iron and zinc form insoluble precipitates in alkaline soils, you can apply iron and zinc salts directly to foliage. You can apply iron and zinc in a chelated form to either soil or foliage.

Nutrient excesses may limit rose growth if the total salt level becomes too high; a value of less than or equal to 2 dS/m is recommended. Plants may show a lack of vigor and short shoots, although no definitive leaf symptoms may occur. However, if salt concentrations are found to be very high (greater than 4 dS/m), you also may see marginal browning or browning of the entire leaves.

A few nutrients cause specific toxicities. Boron can reach high levels in some California soils; an excess causes stunting of plants, chlorosis, and marginal browning of the newest leaves. A soil concentration of less than or equal to 1 part per million is recommended.

Herbicide damage may manifest itself in a variety of symptoms, which include cupped, curled, or yellowed leaves; small leaves; or death of the entire plant. The herbicide class and dosage to the plant determine which symptoms appear and their severity. Injury from glyphosate (e.g., Roundup) is relatively common.

Damage symptoms from glyphosate may not appear during the application season, especially if the application occurred in autumn, but may appear the following spring as a proliferation of small shoots and leaves from buds (fig. 44). The plant will outgrow the injury if the dosage was not too high.

Figure 44. Injury from a glyphosate (e.g., Roundup) herbicide has caused the rose on the left to develop a pale, underdeveloped blossom and puckered, needlelike shoots.

Symptoms on Flower Petals and Buds

Botrytis blight, caused by the fungus *Botrytis cinerea*, thrives in high humidity (fig. 45). Affected plants have spotted flower petals and buds that fail to open, often with woolly, gray fungal spores on decaying tissue. Twigs die back, and large, diffuse, targetlike splotches form on canes.

Lessen humidity around plants by modifying irrigation and pruning techniques and reducing ground cover. Remove and dispose of fallen leaves and petals and prune out infested canes, buds, and flowers. Botrytis blight is a problem usually only during spring and fall in most of California and during summer along coastal areas when the climate is cool and foggy.

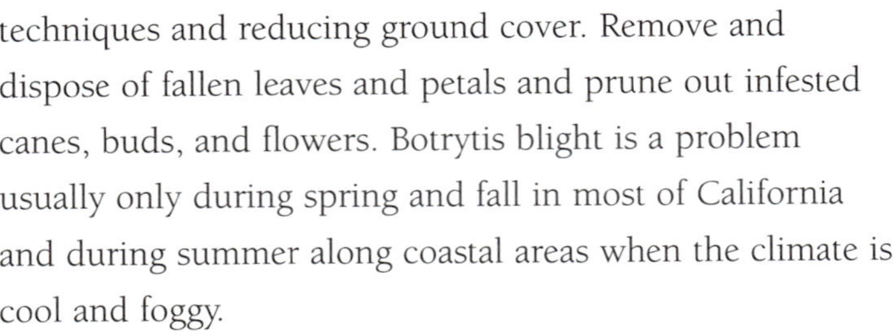

Figure 45. A serious infection of botrytis blight causes blossoms to turn brown and twigs to die back.

Rose phyllody is a flower abnormality recognized for more than 200 years in which leaflike structures replace flower organs (fig. 46). The fundamental cause seems to be changes in plant hormone balance brought about by abiotic conditions such as environmental stress or living infectious agents. Some rose varieties such as floribundas are more likely to exhibit phyllody symptoms, probably due to genetic susceptibility. In fact, one floribunda ancestor is *Rosa chinenis*, from which came the "Green Rose," a curious variety that has a stable mutation causing phyllody in all its flowers.

Phytoplasmas and viruses can disrupt normal hormone production, inducing phyllody in many plant species, but play less important roles in rose phyllody. Although a few reports exist of rose phyllody caused by phytoplasmas, the association is poorly documented. Rose rosette disease, believed to be caused by a virus vectored by the eriophyid mite *Phyllocoptes fructiplilus*, also is reported to cause phyllody of rose blossoms. Insects—most often leafhoppers—can spread these diseases, so the appearance of phyllody often raises concerns about possible disease spread through the garden.

However, in roses the most common cause of phyllody is environmental stress, such as hot weather when flower buds are forming or water stress. If environmental factors are the cause, affected plants usually have normal and abnormal flowers simultaneously but otherwise look healthy. When the weather cools, the plant resumes producing normal flowers.

Rose growers familiar with the characteristics of individual varieties can assess whether phyllody is caused by disease or environmental stress by carefully examining plants. A lack of stunting or yellowing and good overall growth indicate a virus or phytoplasma likely is not the cause; instead, an individual flower is probably responding to specific environmental conditions.

No management practices are suggested other than pruning out individual blooms.

Cankers or Growths on Canes

Botrytis blight, as described above, can cause twig dieback and blotches on canes. A number of different fungi can cause stem cankers and dieback. Cankers are brown, often with gray centers or small, black, spore-producing structures on dead tissue.

It is important to provide proper care to keep plants vigorous to prevent problems. Prune out diseased or dead tissue, making cuts at an angle in healthy tissue just above a node, and avoid wounding canes. Cankers often develop after cold temperature injury, so early spring pruning may not effectively eliminate them if late frosts occur; additional late spring pruning may be necessary.

Winter injury from cold temperatures results in dead or dying flowers, twigs, and stems. A thick layer of leaf mulch may protect roses during the winter in cold mountain areas. Stem canker diseases caused by pathogens that move into injured tissue may follow winter injury.

Sunburn appears as blackened areas, especially on the south and west sides of canes. Excessive temperatures on rose canes cause sunburn, usually as an indirect result of drought stress or spider mite pressure, which caused defoliation. Reflected heat from masonry, vinyl siding, or rock mulch can also cause canes to sunburn.

Crown gall, caused by the bacterium *Agrobacterium tumefaciens,* affects many woody plants, including fruit trees, ornamentals, and roses as well as some herbaceous plants such as chrysanthemums and daisies. Crown gall bacteria invade tissue after wounding. Galls in the form of large, distorted tissue growth form at the base of the cane or sometimes on roots or farther up on stems. Infected canes can be stunted and discolored. It is very difficult to rid plants of crown gall once infected. Do not plant susceptible plants in infested soil or near infected plants. Purchase and plant only high quality stock.

Figure 46. The leaf-like abnormalities in the center of this rose are symptoms of phyllody.

References

Dreistadt, S. H. 2004. Pests of landscape trees and shrubs. Oakland: University of California Division of Agriculture and Natural Resources Publication 3359.

Elmore, C. L., J. J. Stapleton, C. E. Bell, and J. DeVay. 1997. Soil solarization: A nonpesticidal method for controlling diseases, nematodes, and weeds. Oakland: University of California Division of Agriculture and Natural Resources Publication 21377.

Flint, M. L., and S. H. Dreistadt. 1998. Natural enemies handbook. Oakland: University of California Division of Agriculture and Natural Resources Publication 3386.

Flint, M. L., and J. F. Karlik. 2008. Pest notes: Roses in the garden and landscape—Insect and mite pests and beneficials. Oakland: University of California Division of Agriculture and Natural Resources Publication 7466. UC IPM Web site, http://www.ipm.ucdavis.edu/PMG/PESTNOTES/pn7466.html.

Gubler, W. D., and S. T. Koike. 2009. Pest notes: Powdery mildew on ornamentals. Oakland: University of California Division of Agriculture and Natural Resources Publication 7493. UC IPM Web site, http://www.ipm.ucdavis.edu/PMG/PESTNOTES/pn7493.html.

Horst, R. K. 1983. Compendium of rose diseases. St. Paul: APS Press.

Karlik, J. F. 1998. Weed management for roses in landscape plantings. Proceedings of the 50th Annual California Weed Science Society, 12–14.

Karlik, J. F. 2008. Pest notes: Roses in the garden and landscape—Cultural practices and weed control. Oakland: University of California Division of Agriculture and Natural Resources Publication 7465. UC IPM Web site, http://www.ipm.ucdavis.edu/PMG/PESTNOTES/pn7465.html.

Karlik, J. F., and M. L. Flint. 1999. Pest notes: Roses in the garden and landscape–Diseases and abiotic disorders. Oakland: University of California Division of Agriculture and Natural Resources Publication 7463. UC IPM Web site, http://www.ipm.ucdavis.edu/PMG/PESTNOTES/pn7463.html.

Karlik, J. F., and C. Harwood. 1991. Landscape roses bred for performance. California Landscape Magazine 16(3): 28–29.

Karlik, J. F., and S. A. Tjosvold. 2003a. Integrated pest management (IPM) for roses. In A. V. Roberts, ed., Encyclopedia of rose science. Amsterdam, Netherlands: Elsevier Science.

———. 2003b. Spider mites. In A. V. Roberts, ed., Encyclopedia of rose science. Amsterdam, Netherlands: Elsevier Science.

Karlik, J., P. B. Goodell, and G. W. Osteen. 1995. Improved mite sampling may reduce acaricide use in roses. California Agriculture 49(3): 38–40.

Pemberton, H. B., ed. 2007. Proceedings of the Fourth International Symposium on Rose Research and Cultivation. Acta Horticulturae No. 751. International Society for Horticultural Science.

Salem, N., D. Golino, B. Falk, and A. Rowhani. 2008. Identification and partial characterization of a new luteovirus associated with rose spring dwarf disease. Plant Disease 92:508–512.

Wilen, C. A., and C. L. Elmore. 2007. Pest notes: Weed management in landscapes. Oakland: University of California Division of Agriculture and Natural Resources Publication 7441. UC IPM Web site, http://www.ipm.ucdavis.edu/PMG/PESTNOTES/pn7441.html.